December

Week 52

○ **27. MONDAY**

PRIORITIES

○ **28. TUESDAY**

○ **29. WEDNESDAY**

TO DO

○ **30. THURSDAY**

○ **31. FRIDAY**

○ **1. SATURDAY / 2. SUNDAY**

January

○ 3. MONDAY

PRIORITIES

○ 4. TUESDAY

○ 5. WEDNESDAY

TO DO

○ 6. THURSDAY

○ 7. FRIDAY

○ 8. SATURDAY / 9. SUNDAY

January

○ 10. MONDAY

PRIORITIES

○ 11. TUESDAY

○ 12. WEDNESDAY

TO DO

○ 13. THURSDAY

○ 14. FRIDAY

○ 15. SATURDAY / 16. SUNDAY

January

Week 3   01/17/22 – 01/23/22

○ 17. MONDAY

PRIORITIES

○ 18. TUESDAY

○ 19. WEDNESDAY

TO DO

○ 20. THURSDAY

○ 21. FRIDAY

○ 22. SATURDAY / 23. SUNDAY

January

○ 24. MONDAY

PRIORITIES

○ 25. TUESDAY

○ 26. WEDNESDAY

TO DO

○ 27. THURSDAY

○ 28. FRIDAY

○ 29. SATURDAY / 30. SUNDAY

January

○ 31. MONDAY

PRIORITIES

○ 1. TUESDAY

○ 2. WEDNESDAY

TO DO

○ 3. THURSDAY

○ 4. FRIDAY

○ 5. SATURDAY / 6. SUNDAY

February

○ 7. MONDAY

PRIORITIES

○ 8. TUESDAY

○ 9. WEDNESDAY

TO DO

○ 10. THURSDAY

○ 11. FRIDAY

○ 12. SATURDAY / 13. SUNDAY

February

○ 14. MONDAY

PRIORITIES

○ 15. TUESDAY

○ 16. WEDNESDAY

TO DO

○ 17. THURSDAY

○ 18. FRIDAY

○ 19. SATURDAY / 20. SUNDAY

February

○ 21. MONDAY

PRIORITIES

○ 22. TUESDAY

○ 23. WEDNESDAY

TO DO

○ 24. THURSDAY

○ 25. FRIDAY

○ 26. SATURDAY / 27. SUNDAY

February

Week 9   02/28/22 - 03/06/22

○ 28. MONDAY

PRIORITIES

○ 1. TUESDAY

○ 2. WEDNESDAY

TO DO

○ 3. THURSDAY

○ 4. FRIDAY

○ 5. SATURDAY / 6. SUNDAY

March

03/07/22 – 03/13/22

○ 7. MONDAY

PRIORITIES

○ 8. TUESDAY

○ 9. WEDNESDAY

TO DO

○ 10. THURSDAY

○ 11. FRIDAY

○ 12. SATURDAY / 13. SUNDAY

March

○ 14. MONDAY

PRIORITIES

○ 15. TUESDAY

○ 16. WEDNESDAY

TO DO

○ 17. THURSDAY

○ 18. FRIDAY

○ 19. SATURDAY / 20. SUNDAY

March

○ 21. MONDAY

PRIORITIES

○ 22. TUESDAY

○ 23. WEDNESDAY

TO DO

○ 24. THURSDAY

○ 25. FRIDAY

○ 26. SATURDAY / 27. SUNDAY

March

○ 28. MONDAY

PRIORITIES

○ 29. TUESDAY

○ 30. WEDNESDAY

TO DO

○ 31. THURSDAY

○ 1. FRIDAY

○ 2. SATURDAY / 3. SUNDAY

April

○ 4. MONDAY

PRIORITIES

○ 5. TUESDAY

○ 6. WEDNESDAY

TO DO

○ 7. THURSDAY

○ 8. FRIDAY

○ 9. SATURDAY / 10. SUNDAY

April

○ 11. MONDAY

                                        PRIORITIES

○ 12. TUESDAY

○ 13. WEDNESDAY

                                        TO DO

○ 14. THURSDAY

○ 15. FRIDAY

○ 16. SATURDAY / 17. SUNDAY

April

○ **18. MONDAY**

PRIORITIES

○ **19. TUESDAY**

○ **20. WEDNESDAY**

TO DO

○ **21. THURSDAY**

○ **22. FRIDAY**

○ **23. SATURDAY / 24. SUNDAY**

April

○ 25. MONDAY

PRIORITIES

○ 26. TUESDAY

○ 27. WEDNESDAY

TO DO

○ 28. THURSDAY

○ 29. FRIDAY

○ 30. SATURDAY / 1. SUNDAY

May

Week 18

05/02/22 – 05/08/22

○ 2. MONDAY

PRIORITIES

○ 3. TUESDAY

○ 4. WEDNESDAY

TO DO

○ 5. THURSDAY

○ 6. FRIDAY

○ 7. SATURDAY / 8. SUNDAY

May

○ 9. MONDAY

PRIORITIES

○ 10. TUESDAY

○ 11. WEDNESDAY

TO DO

○ 12. THURSDAY

○ 13. FRIDAY

○ 14. SATURDAY / 15. SUNDAY

May

05/16/22 – 05/22/22

○ 16. MONDAY

PRIORITIES

○ 17. TUESDAY

○ 18. WEDNESDAY

TO DO

○ 19. THURSDAY

○ 20. FRIDAY

○ 21. SATURDAY / 22. SUNDAY

May

05/23/22 - 05/29/22

○ 23. MONDAY

PRIORITIES

○ 24. TUESDAY

○ 25. WEDNESDAY

TO DO

○ 26. THURSDAY

○ 27. FRIDAY

○ 28. SATURDAY / 29. SUNDAY

May

Week 22   05/30/22 - 06/05/22

○ 30. MONDAY

                                            PRIORITIES

○ 31. TUESDAY

○ 1. WEDNESDAY

                                            TO DO

○ 2. THURSDAY

○ 3. FRIDAY

○ 4. SATURDAY / 5. SUNDAY

June

Week 23   **06/06/22 - 06/12/22**

○ 6. MONDAY

PRIORITIES

_____

_____

_____

_____

○ 7. TUESDAY

_____

_____

_____

_____

○ 8. WEDNESDAY

TO DO

_____

_____

○ 9. THURSDAY

_____

_____

_____

_____

○ 10. FRIDAY

_____

_____

_____

_____

○ 11. SATURDAY / 12. SUNDAY

_____

_____

_____

_____

June

○ **13. MONDAY**

PRIORITIES

○ **14. TUESDAY**

○ **15. WEDNESDAY**

TO DO

○ **16. THURSDAY**

○ **17. FRIDAY**

○ **18. SATURDAY / 19. SUNDAY**

June

Week 25   06/20/22 - 06/26/22

○ **20. MONDAY**

PRIORITIES

_____
_____
_____
_____

○ **21. TUESDAY**

_____
_____
_____

○ **22. WEDNESDAY**

TO DO

_____
_____

○ **23. THURSDAY**

_____
_____
_____
_____
_____

○ **24. FRIDAY**

_____
_____
_____
_____

○ **25. SATURDAY / 26. SUNDAY**

_____
_____
_____
_____

June

○ 27. MONDAY

PRIORITIES

○ 28. TUESDAY

○ 29. WEDNESDAY

TO DO

○ 30. THURSDAY

○ 1. FRIDAY

○ 2. SATURDAY / 3. SUNDAY

July

07/04/22 – 07/10/22

○ 4. MONDAY

PRIORITIES

○ 5. TUESDAY

○ 6. WEDNESDAY

TO DO

○ 7. THURSDAY

○ 8. FRIDAY

○ 9. SATURDAY / 10. SUNDAY

July

Week 28

○ 11. MONDAY

PRIORITIES

○ 12. TUESDAY

○ 13. WEDNESDAY

TO DO

○ 14. THURSDAY

○ 15. FRIDAY

○ 16. SATURDAY / 17. SUNDAY

July

○ 18. MONDAY

PRIORITIES

○ 19. TUESDAY

○ 20. WEDNESDAY

TO DO

○ 21. THURSDAY

○ 22. FRIDAY

○ 23. SATURDAY / 24. SUNDAY

July

Week 30

○ **25. MONDAY**

PRIORITIES

○ **26. TUESDAY**

○ **27. WEDNESDAY**

TO DO

○ **28. THURSDAY**

○ **29. FRIDAY**

○ **30. SATURDAY / 31. SUNDAY**

August

08/01/22 - 08/07/22

○ 1. MONDAY

PRIORITIES

_____
_____
_____
_____
_____
_____
_____

○ 2. TUESDAY

○ 3. WEDNESDAY

TO DO

_____
_____
_____
_____
_____
_____
_____

○ 4. THURSDAY

○ 5. FRIDAY

_____
_____
_____
_____

○ 6. SATURDAY / 7. SUNDAY

_____
_____
_____
_____

August

08/08/22 – 08/14/22

○ 8. MONDAY

PRIORITIES

○ 9. TUESDAY

○ 10. WEDNESDAY

TO DO

○ 11. THURSDAY

○ 12. FRIDAY

○ 13. SATURDAY / 14. SUNDAY

August

○ 15. MONDAY

PRIORITIES

○ 16. TUESDAY

○ 17. WEDNESDAY

TO DO

○ 18. THURSDAY

○ 19. FRIDAY

○ 20. SATURDAY / 21. SUNDAY

August

○ 22. MONDAY

PRIORITIES

○ 23. TUESDAY

○ 24. WEDNESDAY

TO DO

○ 25. THURSDAY

○ 26. FRIDAY

○ 27. SATURDAY / 28. SUNDAY

August

08/29/22 – 09/04/22

○ 29. MONDAY

PRIORITIES

○ 30. TUESDAY

○ 31. WEDNESDAY

TO DO

○ 1. THURSDAY

○ 2. FRIDAY

○ 3. SATURDAY / 4. SUNDAY

September

○ 5. MONDAY

PRIORITIES

○ 6. TUESDAY

○ 7. WEDNESDAY

TO DO

○ 8. THURSDAY

○ 9. FRIDAY

○ 10. SATURDAY / 11. SUNDAY

September

09/12/22 – 09/18/22

○ 12. MONDAY

PRIORITIES

○ 13. TUESDAY

○ 14. WEDNESDAY

TO DO

○ 15. THURSDAY

○ 16. FRIDAY

○ 17. SATURDAY / 18. SUNDAY

September

09/19/22 - 09/25/22

○ 19. MONDAY

PRIORITIES

○ 20. TUESDAY

○ 21. WEDNESDAY

TO DO

○ 22. THURSDAY

○ 23. FRIDAY

○ 24. SATURDAY / 25. SUNDAY

September

09/26/22 – 10/02/22

○ 26. MONDAY

PRIORITIES

○ 27. TUESDAY

○ 28. WEDNESDAY

TO DO

○ 29. THURSDAY

○ 30. FRIDAY

○ 1. SATURDAY / 2. SUNDAY

October

Week 40   10/03/22 - 10/09/22

○ 3. MONDAY

PRIORITIES

_____

_____

○ 4. TUESDAY

_____

_____

_____

_____

○ 5. WEDNESDAY

TO DO

_____

_____

○ 6. THURSDAY

_____

_____

_____

_____

○ 7. FRIDAY

_____

_____

_____

_____

○ 8. SATURDAY / 9. SUNDAY

_____

_____

_____

October

○ 10. MONDAY

PRIORITIES

○ 11. TUESDAY

○ 12. WEDNESDAY

TO DO

○ 13. THURSDAY

○ 14. FRIDAY

○ 15. SATURDAY / 16. SUNDAY

October

○ 17. MONDAY

PRIORITIES

○ 18. TUESDAY

○ 19. WEDNESDAY

TO DO

○ 20. THURSDAY

○ 21. FRIDAY

○ 22. SATURDAY / 23. SUNDAY

October

Week 43

10/24/22 – 10/30/22

○ 24. MONDAY

PRIORITIES

○ 25. TUESDAY

○ 26. WEDNESDAY

TO DO

○ 27. THURSDAY

○ 28. FRIDAY

○ 29. SATURDAY / 30. SUNDAY

October

○ 31. MONDAY

PRIORITIES

○ 1. TUESDAY

○ 2. WEDNESDAY

TO DO

○ 3. THURSDAY

○ 4. FRIDAY

○ 5. SATURDAY / 6. SUNDAY

November

○ **7. MONDAY**

PRIORITIES

○ **8. TUESDAY**

○ **9. WEDNESDAY**

TO DO

○ **10. THURSDAY**

○ **11. FRIDAY**

○ **12. SATURDAY / 13. SUNDAY**

November

○ 14. MONDAY

PRIORITIES

○ 15. TUESDAY

○ 16. WEDNESDAY

TO DO

○ 17. THURSDAY

○ 18. FRIDAY

○ 19. SATURDAY / 20. SUNDAY

November

○ 21. MONDAY

PRIORITIES

○ 22. TUESDAY

○ 23. WEDNESDAY

TO DO

○ 24. THURSDAY

○ 25. FRIDAY

○ 26. SATURDAY / 27. SUNDAY

November

11/28/22 – 12/04/22

○ 28. MONDAY

PRIORITIES

○ 29. TUESDAY

○ 30. WEDNESDAY

TO DO

○ 1. THURSDAY

○ 2. FRIDAY

○ 3. SATURDAY / 4. SUNDAY

December

12/05/22 – 12/11/22

○ 5. MONDAY

PRIORITIES

○ 6. TUESDAY

○ 7. WEDNESDAY

TO DO

○ 8. THURSDAY

○ 9. FRIDAY

○ 10. SATURDAY / 11. SUNDAY

December

○ 12. MONDAY

PRIORITIES

○ 13. TUESDAY

○ 14. WEDNESDAY

TO DO

○ 15. THURSDAY

○ 16. FRIDAY

○ 17. SATURDAY / 18. SUNDAY

December

○ **19. MONDAY**

PRIORITIES

_____
_____
_____
_____
_____

○ **20. TUESDAY**

_____
_____

○ **21. WEDNESDAY**

TO DO

_____
_____
_____

○ **22. THURSDAY**

_____
_____
_____
_____

○ **23. FRIDAY**

_____
_____
_____
_____

○ **24. SATURDAY / 25. SUNDAY**

_____
_____
_____
_____

December

12/26/22 – 01/01/23

○ 26. MONDAY

PRIORITIES

_____

_____

○ 27. TUESDAY

_____

_____

_____

_____

_____

_____

○ 28. WEDNESDAY

TO DO

_____

_____

○ 29. THURSDAY

_____

_____

_____

_____

_____

○ 30. FRIDAY

_____

_____

_____

_____

_____

○ 31. SATURDAY / 1. SUNDAY

_____

_____

_____

_____

Made in the USA
Monee, IL
13 July 2021